Project Shine

Building self-esteem
Encouraging self-love
Strengthening family relationships

Jo Ettles

Project Shine
Jo Ettles
Published by Jo Ettles
First published 2018
Email info@joettles.com.au or visit www.joettles.com.au
Copyright © 2018 Jo Ettles
ISBN9780994458391

Editor: Jo Ettles
Designer/ graphics/ typesetter :Tony Ettles
Self -published
Printed by IngramSpark
Author: Ettles, Jo
Title: Project Shine
ISBN: 9780994458391
Subjects: Self-acceptance
                  Self-actualization (Psychology)
                  Conduct of life

"Perhaps they are not stars in the sky, but rather
openings where our loved ones shine down
to let us know that they are happy."
Eskimo Proverb

Project Shine
For Dad

Intention

Nowadays, families come in many variations. Whether blood related or soul connected, family are the people in your life that you share a special and loving bond with. In today's busy world, it is easy to become disconnected; with yourself and each other.

It is important that we make the time to prioritize our self-care in mind, body, and spirit.

Project Shine invites everyone, no matter what their relationship, to join forces and invest in some serious self-esteem building and self-love activities, TOGETHER.

When you set goals with clear intentions and then break them down into manageable tasks and action them with your loved ones, magic happens.

I wish you peace.
The kind that lights you up from the inside.
Jo Ettles

Contents of Project Shine

Receive your daily love note by randomly opening a page.

What is Project Shine?

When I was in my early twenties, I worked as a modeling, deportment and grooming teacher. I worked with children, teenagers, young adults and mature aged men and women. My intention back then was to assist my students to build strong self-esteem.

In my opinion, strong self-esteem is the absolute foundation upon which you can consciously create a positive life. I worked hard to empower my students. I encouraged them to honor themselves, practice healthy habits every single day, and always believe in their own power. Thirty years on and I have changed direction. I now work as a life, wellness and spiritual coach.

Originally, when I started working as a coach, my role was to advise and mentor predominantly women on the benefits of good nutrition as a means to achieving wellness. The more clients I coached, the more I realized the following - **Good health is about so much more than eating salad and drinking green smoothies.**

Over the years, my clients have always shared their struggles openly and honestly with me at sessions. There has been a common thread that has run through almost every single conversation I have ever had. That thread consists of the fact that many of us have the ability to be really unkind to ourselves. We can spend way too much time focussing on what we think is wrong with us and absolutely not enough time focussing on what is right with us.

All my clients have shared similar traits. They are amazing, intelligent, talented, gifted people who radiate warmth and love. Beautiful minds, beautiful hearts, beautiful souls, and yet each and every single one of them sadly is capable of negative self-talk. They have often described in great detail during sessions what they consider to be their faults. It is more common than not that they focus all of their attention on their challenges. Rarely, do they focus on their attributes and positive qualities.

I have often asked my clients when they are in a downward spiral of negative self-talk, **"Would you speak to someone you loved like this?"** Words are so powerful. On one hand, they can uplift, energize and encourage. On the other hand, they can destroy your self-esteem, your relationships, and even your health. As vital as it is to pay attention to how we communicate with others, it is even more important to pay attention to how we speak about ourselves and each other.

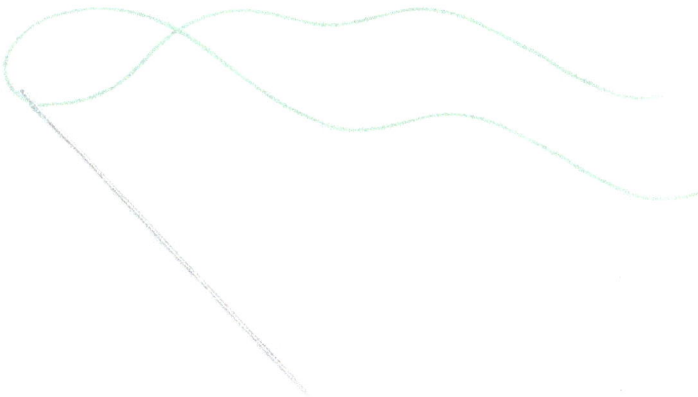

My beautiful clients made me aware of the importance of self-care, positive self-talk and respecting yourself. When this is not a priority, it can impact all areas of your life.

It is not selfish to love, care, and honor yourself. In fact, prioritizing your self-care on every level is one of the greatest ways to show love to your family and friends.

We must love ourselves enough to accept that every day we have the opportunity to shine and if we choose, we can light the way for so many others.

What is Project Shine about?

Project Shine is about
- Love and respect
- Building yourself up
- Building each other up
-Initiating positive changes in mind, body and spirit
- Sharing good energy in your sacred space – your home

Family connections sometimes get strained due to life's crazy pace so the aim of Project Shine is to help you find internal peace and then, in turn, gift that peace to each other.

How to use
Project Shine
Effectively

Decide who will participate in Project Shine. The program is written for adults, older children, and teenagers to complete together. Project Shine is best suited to children twelve years and above, but it depends on the child/teens individual level of maturity. When it comes to growth and self-development, you know your family best. I recommend that you assess the material first and decide if it is suitable or not.

Any number and any combination of family members or friends can take part in the program. For example, a mum plus two kids can work together. A dad and one teen might complete the project. A whole family can share the experience. Aunts, uncles, nieces, nephews, even groups of friends can participate in the project together. You don't have to be related, just connected. There are no restrictions on who can SHINE.

There are eight weeks of personal development with supporting tasks and activities. It is best to work through each chapter consecutively but there are no hard and fast rules. If it suits you to do one chapter per month with your loved ones, or one chapter every two months, then that is fine. For ease and flow, I encourage you to do one chapter a week for eight weeks.

Elect a new task leader when you begin a new chapter if possible. The task leaders role is to ensure that everyone participating in Project Shine is up to speed with all of the information and activities. It is a good idea to schedule a family meeting prior to starting a new chapter. This gives the task leader an opportunity to share the chapter material, the tasks, and activities involved.

Journaling is an important part of Project Shine. It is vital that each person participating in the program invest in a journal or notebook so that they can write their thoughts and feelings into their own private space after completing a chapter.

I encourage you to embrace journaling. It allows you to share your feelings without judgment. It helps to identify unhealthy patterns that may be happening on a daily or weekly basis. It keeps you accountable and it encourages creativity and emotional release.

Who knows, you may enjoy journaling so much that you will incorporate it into your everyday life. Journaling is also another way to share your story with loved ones especially if you struggle to talk about your feelings.

Work on each chapter of Project Shine and complete all of the tasks assigned for that week. Make sure you gather together as often as you can so you can share your progress as well as how you are feeling, growing and SHINING.

In a nutshell….

1.Decide who will participate in Project Shine.

2. Make sure everyone has a journal.

3. Ensure everyone is committed.

4. Be open and honest.

5. Participate fully.

6. Feel free to create and add extra activities to each chapter if you wish.

7. Everyone's ideas, thoughts and feelings are welcome and should be respected especially at family gatherings.

8. Open your heart to mental and spiritual growth.

9. Immerse yourself in the activities.

10. Come from a place of love.

Task leader tips...Always select a task leader upon commencing a new chapter. Use the following tips to guide you forward.

1. Everyone should step up at some point and have a go at being the task leader. If you are nervous about the job at hand, ask everyone to help you lead.

2. SHARE the chapter material with everyone.

3. IDENTIFY and acknowledge the goal for the week.

4. HOW will you achieve this goal? Be sure that everyone understands the material as well as the tasks.

5. COMMUNICATE clearly.

6. WHY should everyone participate? Discuss the positives that will accompany the chapter.

7. DEFINE the timeline for the week

8. WHAT actions will everyone take daily to achieve the goals and activities.

9. COMMIT to honoring yourself and each other fully.

10. STEP UP and lead with confidence.

Creating A Positive Foundation

Family, like branches on a tree, we can all grow in totally different directions but our roots always remain as one.

Invest Structure Maintain

Three important steps when building a solid foundation

When it comes to personal development, an important first step is to examine the foundation that you are about to expand and build upon. A solid foundation is a good basis for anything long lasting.

INVEST

Invest the time and energy into working together on Project Shine. Always schedule a family meeting when commencing a new chapter. This allows everyone to participate fully as well as offer their input on how everyone can best work together on the upcoming activities. By investing time into planning, you are already preparing your foundation. This is an important step when it comes to strengthening your foundation.

STRUCTURE is an important part of any foundation. Your structure should be solid, strong and well connected. Acknowledge together as a family the following question, *Are there any cracks in your foundation?*

Openly and honestly express your feelings and opinions with one another on ways you can repair and strengthen your family's foundation *if* it needs repairing. It is vital to identify any underlying issues so you can work on fixing them.

MAINTAIN your daily routines as best you can. Life isn't perfect and from time to time, cracks will appear in your foundation. It is vital to always regroup, refocus and work towards maintaining your relationships, goals and everyday commitments. Regular maintenance is key when it comes to keeping everything solid and stable.

It is important that everyone who is taking part in Project Shine maintain a commitment to one another regarding completing the activities and tasks assigned. By uniting and completing the whole program, you will create a solid foundation you can continue to grow from.

66

Without a solid foundation, you will have trouble creating and sustaining anything stable and long lasting.

Week 1
Reconnecting

Your goal this week -
To reconnect with one another

Over the next seven days, everyone participating in
Project Shine must complete the following -

The" How well do you know each other" task.

Schedule a family dinner to challenge each other with the
" How well do you know each other" task. Bring your task
answers to the family gathering and have some fun.

Family dinners are a great way to reconnect.
You can schedule more than one dinner if you wish.

Allocate ten minutes every single day this week
to discuss and share at least one positive thing about your
day with each other.

Spend time at the end of the week journaling about this
week's tasks and how you have reconnected with one another.
You can share your journal or keep it private.

Please note-
No phones or electronic devices allowed during any of these
activities. During your family catch-ups, be fully present and
engaged.

Even though you interact with one another regularly, *how well do you really know each other?* Are you aware of each other's likes and dislikes? Do you know what makes each other happy or unhappy?

We all lead extremely busy lives. It is often the case that we might all be sharing the same space but we are existing in separate worlds. When we become disconnected, we can quite literally miss big chunks of each others' lives.

Pay attention to your family. Listen and engage with each other fully. It is really important that we make an effort to communicate openly, honestly and respectfully with one another as often as we can. When we communicate clearly and when we make the effort to connect often, we gain the confidence to be able to express our needs, thoughts, and feelings effectively.

How well do you know each other task

In your journal, answer the task questions as honestly and as openly as you can.

Don't show ANYONE your answers while you are completing the task.

Keep your answers private.

Bring your answers to this week's scheduled family gathering.

The challenge for everyone participating in this week's task is to guess your answers to see just how well they know you.

This is a great way to reconnect and share your likes, dislikes, hopes, and goals for the future.

Your mission with this week's task......
have FUN !!!!

Here are your task questions

What are your favourite foods?

Do you have a favourite color?

Who are your favourite musicians?

What is your favourite song?

What do you do to relax?

What is your favourite way to exercise?

What are you most proud of?

What is one GOAL that you hope to achieve this year?

If you had to prepare a meal for your family,
what would you most likely cook?

Do you have a best friend?

What annoys you?

Do you have any quirky habits?

What makes you laugh?

Reflection and journaling- Week one

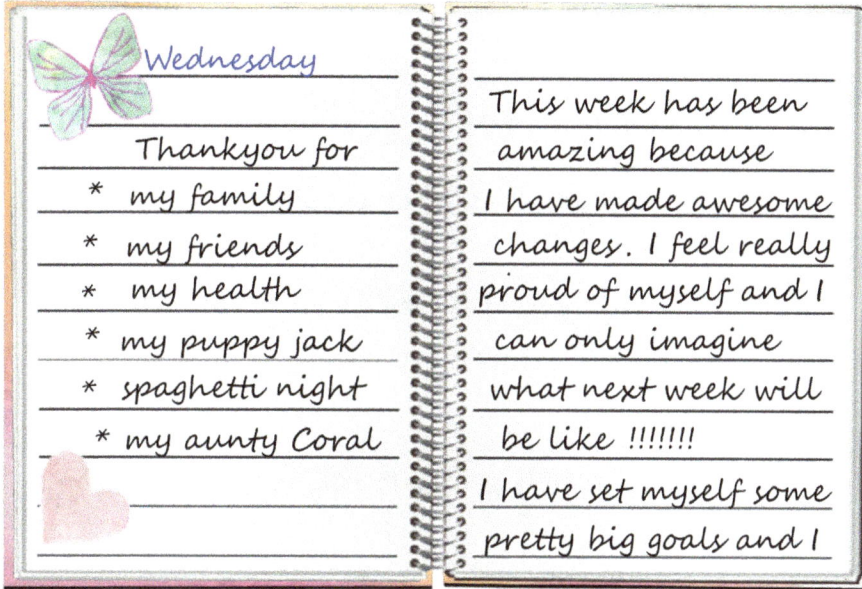

Wednesday

Thankyou for
* my family
* my friends
* my health
* my puppy jack
* spaghetti night
* my aunty Coral

This week has been
amazing because
I have made awesome
changes. I feel really
proud of myself and I
can only imagine
what next week will
be like !!!!!!!
I have set myself some
pretty big goals and I

Journaling and reflecting are good for the soul. Make time this week to fill in your journal. Be open and honest about what you have learned about yourself and each other. You can share your journaling or keep it private. If you have never filled in a journal before, the following questions will guide you and help get you started. The most important aspect of journaling is to write from your heart.

What did you learn about yourself this week?

What did you learn about each other this week?

Do you feel more connected to one another?

What are you grateful for this week?

Connection Tips

Smile at other people.

Really listen when someone is talking to you.

Be totally present - no phones!

Be authentic and totally genuine.

Listen without judgment.

Eye contact is important when you are communicating. It shows the other person that you are interested and tuned in to what they are talking about.

66

Love, belonging and
connection are the universal sources of
true well-being.

Week 2
Building
Self-Esteem

Your goal this week -
To build self-esteem

This chapter is huge, so you may want to complete it over one week or you can extend it out over a few weeks.
Everyone participating in Project Shine must complete the following -

"Today I will acknowledge my strengths, positive qualities and I will celebrate my uniqueness" task.

Plan a family dinner to discuss the results of the above task. This gathering is also an opportunity to support one another and ensure that everybody is up to speed with all of the assigned activities. Schedule more than one family dinner if possible.

Every day this week, you are required to make a small entry into your journal. Please refer to the self-esteem daily journaling task in this chapter for guidance.

Check your self-esteem tank daily and review the self-esteem action points as often as you can.
There is more info about how to do that in this chapter.

Whenever you find yourself thinking negative thoughts this week, review the "Challenge your negative belief points" included in this self-esteem building section and get into the habit of retraining your mind to focus on the positives.

No phones or electronic devices allowed during any of these activities. During your family catch-ups, be fully present and engaged.

Self-esteem is best described as the value we place on ourselves. It is our overall sense of self-worth and it affects our trust in others, our trust in ourselves, our relationships, and our quality of life.

If you think about it, nearly every part of our existence, past, present, and future is influenced by our self-esteem levels.

I want you to place your hands on your solar plexus. Your solar plexus is located just near your belly button. Imagine each one of us is born with an inbuilt self-esteem tank. It is just like the fuel tank in a car. The gauge to this self-esteem tank is located and visible on your forehead…….. (how funny would that be?)

My self-esteem tank

Ok, just for the purpose of this exercise, seriously focus your attention on your solar plexus and connect to this energy center. Visualize your self-esteem tank and imagine that it is located where your hands are placed. (Refer to the image on the previous page.) Imagine that this is where you store all of your self-esteem on a daily basis.

Pretend that there is a sensing unit inside your self-esteem tank and it tracks your self-esteem levels, meanwhile, that funny indicator on your forehead keeps a visible record so that you can monitor whether your tank is full or empty.

When you value yourself, when you are full of confidence and when you appreciate every part of yourself, imagine that the indicator needle (located on your forehead) points to 'F' representing a full tank of self- esteem.

You know you can change the whole world when you have a full tank of self-esteem. It is powerful, contagious and the most valuable form of energy to possess. When this tank is empty though that gauge points to 'E' indicating an empty tank.

When your self-esteem tank is low, you can feel miserable, worthless, scared, tired and drained. Just like a car, you may require someone to give you a push to keep you moving forward.

It is pretty obvious that we do not have a visible self-esteem gauge to rely on, so if we don't pay attention to how we are feeling, we may be running on empty and if that's the case, we may not be reaching our full potential.

Sometimes, you can feel that you are low in self-esteem. You might even feel it draining away but you don't stop often enough to refill your self-esteem tank.

We cannot rely on other people to keep our self-esteem levels high. We are individually responsible for managing this ourselves.

We must acknowledge that our health, happiness, uniqueness and our contributions to the world are important - this is something we all need to take ownership of.

You are not defined by how you look, what size you are, where you come from or what color your hair is!

You are defined by your heart and your mind. Your self-esteem is shaped by your thoughts, actions, contributions and the value you place on all of your personal achievements and attributes.

It is your birthright to have a healthy amount of self-esteem and self-worth and we must acknowledge that each day as we walk this earth; we owe it to ourselves to SHINE.

Perhaps you can discuss the following at your next family gathering.........

Negative self-talk, negative thoughts and spending time with negative people can drain your self-esteem.

What other things can deplete your self-esteem tank?

Sometimes, we just have to let things go…...

Negative self-talk and negative thoughts

Whether you do it verbally or in the recesses of your mind, constantly criticizing, insulting and belittling your own self is one of the fastest ways to drain your self-esteem. Negative thinking can impact your health, relationships and your overall quality of life. It is time to pay attention to your thoughts and your self-talk.

Negative people

Your happiness and self-worth shouldn't be entirely dependent on other people. The truth is though, personal relationships do have an influence on how you feel and that includes how you feel about yourself. Surround yourself with people who inspire you and genuinely care about you.

You know we are all a little bit weird in some way. What sets you apart may seem like somewhat of a burden, but it's not. Most of the time, it's what makes you so incredible and unique.

Everyone deserves love and respect without terms and conditions.

Always be true to yourself. It's ok to be happy with who you are. It's ok to be unapologetically and uniquely YOU.

The world needs more of your individuality and your unique brand of awesomeness and the world needs it now.

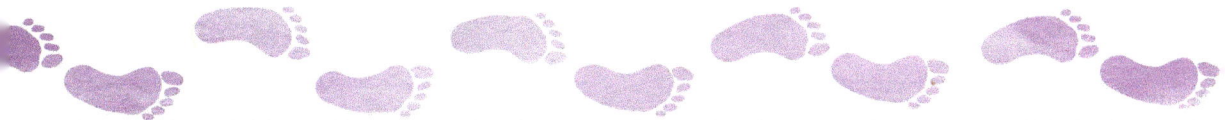

Today I will acknowledge my strengths and positive qualities and I will celebrate my uniqueness task

In your journal, answer the task questions on the next page as honestly as you can.

Be proud of all of your positive qualities and strengths.

This task reminds you to stop and acknowledge everything that is truly wonderful about you.

Discuss this task when it is completed at your family dinner.

Don't be shy about your wonderful qualities and achievements.
Own them!

Your mission with this task......
honor yourself.

Here are your task questions

List three or more things that you are good at.

List three or more things that you LOVE about yourself.

List three or more things that make you uniquely different from everyone else.

List three or more challenges that you have overcome.

What are your strengths?

What are your best qualities?

What amazing things have you achieved to date?

Journaling is good for the soul

For the next seven days, work on building more self-esteem through journaling. Fill in your journal daily.

Use the self-esteem building questions on the next page to guide you. Don't feel restricted by just two questions.

If you want to keep journaling all the positives….go crazy!

Spend at least ten minutes a day on this activity.

Here are your journaling questions for this week

Monday
What is something you did well today?
What inspired pride in you today?

Tuesday
What did you accomplish today?
How positive were you today on a scale of one to ten?

Wednesday
What did you do today that warmed your heart?
Did you feel proud of someone else today?

Thursday
How did you motivate yourself today?
What positive choices did you make today?

Friday
What activities or choices did you make that supported your health and well-being?
What did you do today to inspire change in the people around you?

Saturday and Sunday
What was the best part about the weekend?
What positive changes will you incorporate into the upcoming week?

Journaling Tips

Be open and honest when journaling your thoughts and feelings.

Write from your heart always.

Spend at least ten minutes a day journaling.

Journaling can help you release negative thoughts and it can assist in boosting self-esteem.

Some of the most inspirational thought leaders throughout history journaled about their lives so with that in mind, consider incorporating journaling into your days forever.

Tell yourself the most amazing stories each
and every day. Find the gift in every situation and always
search for the silver lining.
Instead of a good day, have an amazing day.
Instead of feeling well, feel incredibly healthy,
energized and illuminated.
Instead of being good enough, be great enough.
The stories you tell yourself define you and
create your reality.

Challenge your negative beliefs

Work on identifying any of your negative beliefs. As a family, support each other as best you can to shift these beliefs to positive ones. The stories you tell yourself have the potential to define or destroy you, so tell yourself positively, wonderful stories every single day.

There are four main types of questions on the next page that will help you to challenge your negative beliefs. Get familiar with them and ask yourself these questions anytime you need to re-frame your stories. Whenever you are focussing on a negative situation or if you feel worried about something, run the following four sets of reality testing questions. Create a better story about what is occurring.

When you let go of the things that weigh you down, you create space for something better.....

Reality testing questions

1. Reality testing
What is my evidence for and against my thinking?
Am I jumping to negative conclusions?
How can I find out if my thoughts are true and correct?

2. Try to look for alternative explanations
Are there any other ways that I could look at this situation?
What else could this mean?
Am I over thinking this situation?

3. Putting it into perspective
What is the best thing that could result from this situation?
What are the positives in this situation?
Will this matter in five years' time?

4. Use goal-directed thinking
Does this way of thinking help me to achieve my goals?
What can I do that will help me to solve the problem?
What can I learn from this situation, that will help me cope better next time?

Here are your

self-esteem

action points

Action one- Straighten up and stay energized

Poor posture can influence your physical and mental energy. There have been many studies done that support sitting up straight as a way to increase confidence and improve energy levels so...

SIT UP STRAIGHT.

Action two- Review your negative beliefs

Once you believe something negative about yourself, it becomes all-consuming. Always look for evidence to disprove your negative beliefs. Ask yourself, is this belief helpful? Where did this limiting belief come from? What would you rather believe instead? Use the reality testing questions as a guide.

Action three- Accept yourself as you are

Look in the mirror every morning and say "I love and approve of myself." You may feel uncomfortable with this at first but do it every day until you can look yourself in the eyes and mean what you say.

Action four- Immerse yourself in positivity

Listen to motivational talks, read self-development books, attend self-help events and workshops. Whatever thoughts you allow to dominate your mind will eventually take root and affect your behavior. Set aside time every day for personal development.

Action five- Don't compare yourself to others

Do you compare your life to other people's lives? Let me remind you that this serves no purpose. Focus on your own strengths and be proud of all of *your* achievements. Do not waste time and energy comparing yourself to anyone else. The only person you should compete against is yourself.

Action six- Don't hash over past mistakes

Absolutely, everyone makes mistakes. When something doesn't work out, don't stress or worry about it, instead, learn from it and move on. While you are at it, don't be afraid to apologize if you need to. Apologizing is not always easy but if you need to say sorry to someone, do it from the heart. It is healing and shows integrity and strength.

Action seven - Focus on the things you *can* change

If you feel overwhelmed and if everything in your world feels chaotic, there's no point wasting all of your time and energy focussing on the things that you *can't* change. Shift your attention to what you *can* change and then start making small, positive changes every day.

Action eight-Surround yourself with supportive people

Always surround yourself with people who make you feel good about yourself. Avoid the ones who bring you down. Mix with positive, upbeat and inspiring people who energize you and appreciate your positive qualities. When you surround yourself with people who accept and encourage you, your self-esteem will stay firmly intact.

Action nine- Do more of what you LOVE every single day
When we partake in activities we enjoy, it boosts our happiness which is perfect for improving our self-esteem levels.

Action ten - Quit worrying about everything and anything
If you make a list of all the things you are worried about today and then put your list away, chances are that when you come back to it in a week or two, you'll discover that most, if not all the things you were worried about, never happened. DON'T waste your precious energy on worrying!

Today is a perfect day to let go of the things that no longer serve you.....

Reflection and journaling- Week two

Friday

I am grateful for
* The weekend
* Family dinner
* My nice warm bed
* Mum and dad
* Not having to
study this weekend

chocolate!!! lol

I am feeling
so much better about
myself. I am important
and no-one has the
right to make me feel
like I am not.
This week I have
experienced a big
shift in my self-esteem
and I am looking for

This has been a BIG week of self-discovery. It is important to make time now for reflection. Be open and honest about what you have learned and how you are feeling about this past week's activities. You can share your journaling or keep it private. Use the following questions to guide you.

What did you learn about yourself this week?

Has your self-esteem improved?

What will you do each day to improve your self-esteem?

What are you grateful for this week?

"

You did not wake up today to
be mediocre -
Give yourself permission
to SHINE.

Week 3

Lift Each Other Up

Your goal this week-
To acknowledge each other's strengths

Over the next seven days, everyone participating in
Project Shine must complete the following -

Select a family member who is participating in Project Shine.

Your task is to write a letter to this person acknowledging all
of your favourite things about them. If you wish to write a
letter to more than one family member, go for it.

Remember, there are no hard rules. If it feels right to
change things up, then change away.

Schedule a family dinner
and either present your letter to your loved one or better
still, read it out loud to this person.

Practice some serious heart hugging this week.
Heart hug at least once a day or whenever the opportunity
arises.

No phones or electronic devices allowed during any of these
activities. During your family catch-ups, be fully present and
engaged.

If you want to lift YOURSELF up...
then lift someone ELSE up

Sometimes, families are complicated and when we are busy, we can take each other for granted. From this day forward, let's commit to focussing on each other's strengths and positive qualities. During week three, your task/ activity is all about letter writing. Select a family member and then write them a letter. This letter acknowledges all of your favourite things about your loved one.

Honor your loved one by acknowledging all the things you admire and respect about them. By writing this in letter format, your loved one has a copy to treasure forever. When words are heartfelt, they have the power to heal, uplift, reconnect and even repair the most damaged of relationships. Use your words in this letter writing activity to express your love and appreciation. Words of gratitude are priceless.

Write your family member a letter
to treasure forever

Your mission with this task…..
Write as many pages as you like and fill these pages with
words that express your feelings about your loved one.

Dear_____

I love you because ………

I am grateful to you because ………

Thank you for …………

You are special to me because…….

I admire you because…………

With love and respect from this day forward

Signed_____

Heart Hugs

It is often in our most challenging of times that we react irrationally rather than respond with clarity. Emotions are amplified when we are under stress and it is easy to become overwhelmed.

It can be difficult to stay grounded when you feel like the ground is shaking beneath you but remember, it can be just as difficult for a loved one to watch you struggle.

Sometimes, there aren't any words that can soothe or settle heartache. When you find yourself at a loss for words, hug someone.

When a loved one, a child or a dear friend hugs *you,* when you snuggle up with your beloved pets, your body releases oxytocin. Often referred to as the love hormone, it helps to make us feel warm, fuzzy and less stressed.

A beautiful, warm hug will often provide more comfort and support than a million words and it is a powerful way to heal and connect. The powerful energy exchange between those hugging is a loving investment into the relationship.

It strengthens our immune function. It can help to relieve stress, It relaxes us and allows us to give and receive love unconditionally.

Your task is to heart hug each other every day this week. Schedule at least one heart hug a day or just do it when you see an opportunity to connect.

How to heart hug

If we lean in left shoulder to left shoulder when we embrace someone, we allow our heart energy to connect.

By touching our left-sides together, we share our heart emotions, feelings, and our love. This is a profound shift from hugging on our right-sides, where we share the emotions of our livers. This is where anger, resentment, and pain is stored. By connecting our right-sides, we connect the negative and unhappy aspects of ourselves.

When we connect and embrace left side to left side, we are strengthening our heart connections, and it is a powerful and beautiful way to transfer love – heart to heart.

As part of this week's task, I encourage you to practice heart hugging as often as you can. If it feels uncomfortable, try to let go of any fear and just relax into it.

Feel the connection and use this hugging time as an opportunity to strengthen connections between one another.

The benefits of a beautiful hug….

Hugging comforts us.

Hugging makes us feel relaxed.

Hugging boosts oxytocin which helps to
ease stress.

Hugging lowers blood pressure and
reduces the levels of the harmful stress hormone
cortisol.

Hugging lifts serotonin levels,
elevating our mood and making us feel happier.

Reflection and journaling - Week 3

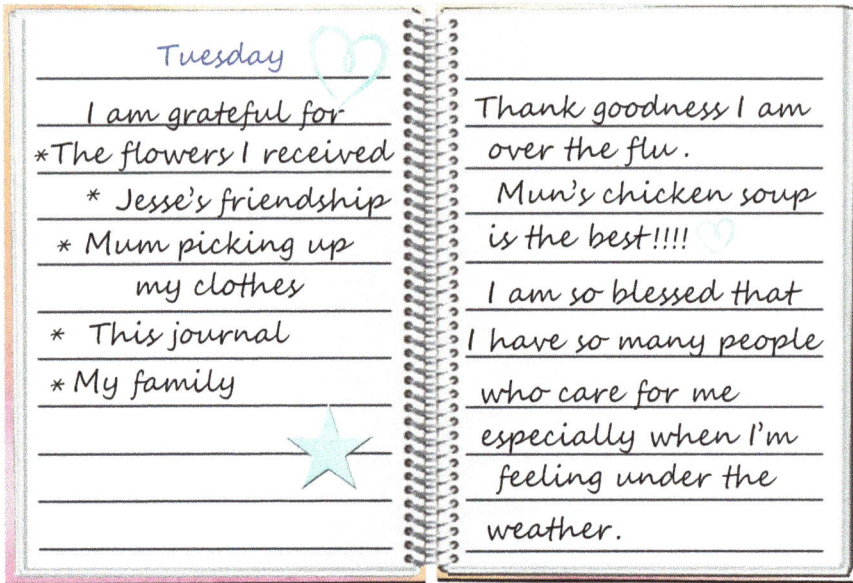

Tuesday

I am grateful for
* The flowers I received
* Jesse's friendship
* Mum picking up
  my clothes
* This journal
* My family

Thank goodness I am
over the flu.
  Mum's chicken soup
is the best!!!!
I am so blessed that
I have so many people
who care for me
especially when I'm
feeling under the
weather.

Invest time now into reflection and journaling.
Be open and honest about what you have learned and how
you are feeling. You can share your journaling or keep it
private. Use the following questions to guide you.

What did you learn about yourself this week?

What did you learn about each other?

Do you feel uplifted?

What did you enjoy most about this week's activities?

What are you grateful for this week?

"

Connect to each other
to connect to your soul.

Week 4
Self-Love

Your goal this week-
Participate in the seven daily acts of self-love

Over the next seven days, everyone participating in Project Shine must complete the following –

Schedule a family dinner at the beginning of the week. During this catch-up, get acquainted with the seven daily acts of self-love.

Plan at least one activity for every day that relates to the seven acts. Everyone must participate.
Use your imagination and create an activity that everyone will enjoy.

If it is difficult to do one act per day,
then extend the seven acts out over two or three weeks.
The most important thing is to incorporate these acts into your life on a regular basis.

No phones or electronic devices allowed during any of these activities. During your family catch-ups, be fully present and engaged.

What is self-love?

Self-love is a deep appreciation and respect for
who we are in mind, body, and spirit.
You can't buy self-love and you can't get it from
anyone else. You can increase it by practicing daily
habits that support physical, mental and
spiritual growth and expansion.
Maintaining a healthy sense of self-love
is crucial to your overall well-being.

We travel through life forming and reforming hundreds of relationships. Friends, colleagues, relatives, peers, and what we learn from these connections and interactions ultimately, is that anyone may come and go at any given moment into our lives, absolutely anyone, but there is only one relationship that endures as a permanent fixture throughout the entirety of your life, and that is the relationship you have with yourself.

If the relationship with yourself is strained, then your external bonds and your whole quality of life are bound to suffer.

Maintaining a healthy sense of self-love is crucial to your overall well-being. The more you nourish, accept, understand, and appreciate yourself, the more you will thrive under any circumstance.

The seven daily acts of self-love remind you to love, care and honor yourself.

Your mission with this task...............
do something every single day that fills your mind, body and spirit with love and light.

Here are
your seven
daily acts

Act one- Practice healthy habits

Nourish yourself daily with good, healthy and nutritious food. Move more and ensure you get enough rest and good quality sleep. Always engage in healthy social interactions.

Acknowledge together as a family the following question. Do you need to eliminate any unhealthy habits? For example, are you drinking too much soft drink or eating a lot of unhealthy takeaway foods? Are you spending hours in front of the gogglebox or engaging in way too much social media consumption? What about swearing, bad manners, toxic relationships? It is important to identify all of your unhealthy habits first so you can begin the process of eliminating them.

Once you have done this, make a commitment to replace these negative habits with healthy habits. Keep each other accountable when it comes to making better choices. What will you do this week to support act one?

Act two- Nourish your spirit

Make time for a leisurely stroll at sunset or consider a barefoot walk along the beach. Maybe you could explore a forest or national park. If the weather permits, take a dip in the ocean.

Listen to a guided meditation, practice earthing or grounding. Earthing or grounding is when you lay on the grass or any patch of earth and connect to it. There is extensive research to support that just twenty minutes of grounding and connecting to the earth every day can bring many positive benefits.

Factor in time every week to do more things that make you feel alive. Slow down and nourish your spirit. This is a perfect way to reconnect with yourself. What will you do this week to support act two?

Act three-Honor your living space

Create an organized, peaceful and calming living space for yourself and your family. Your home is your safe haven and it is where you retreat to recharge your batteries every single day. It is a place to gather - to love, listen, celebrate and support one another. Declutter areas of your home that are in chaos and aim for simplicity and flow. Start with one room at a time. Discard unnecessary stuff and let go of anything you don't use or need. Be honest and not emotional when deciding what you will keep or discard.

If this seems like an overwhelming job, consider clearing one room per month until everything feels zen-like. When you have completed decluttering and your home's energy is flowing, honor your space with scented candles, flowers, and greenery. Always be responsible for keeping your living space in good order. Your home is your sanctuary. Make sure you fill it with love, peace, and warmth. What will you do this week to support act three?

Act four- Be spontaneous

We all have responsibilities and commitments. When our lives are super busy, often the only way to get through it all is by following a strict routine.

I want to remind you that life is for living. Don't be so rigid with your routines and schedules that there is no time left to play or seize the many magical moments that exist. Live your life with purpose and with intention. Set goals and have big dreams for the future, but also remember that life is best lived in the present moment.

With that in mind, don't be afraid to do something spontaneous. Go see a movie or enjoy a special picnic dinner at the beach or the park. Come up with some activity that will break up your routine. Change things up and pay attention to how alive it makes you feel. What will you do this week to support act four?

Act five- Practice mindfulness

Life becomes AMPLIFIED when you're in the present moment, so with that in mind, designate a specific time during your day to focus on what's happening around you or in front of you.

Close your eyes, place your hands on your solar plexus and take three deep breaths in and out.

Now pay attention……………….
What can you hear? What can you smell? How do you feel?

It's impossible to live in a state of bliss all the time. The reality is that the world we live in doesn't always allow for that. But anytime you feel disconnected from yourself and/or your family, unplug and tune into what is happening around you and in you. What will you do this week to support act five?

Act six- Unplug and smell the roses

Commit to detoxing from technology often. This means that we should turn off mobile phones and computers for a specific period of time every day. Yes, that's right. I said every single day!

When you commit to a daily dose of unplugging, you will allow your mind to reboot and that is priceless.

By reducing the number of mindless activities we indulge in, like checking your phone, scrolling through social media, watching silly clips on YouTube, and replacing them with activities that require you to invest in yourself or each other, you'll be amazed at how much energy you cultivate. You will also notice how much better you feel and how productive you become. What will you do this week to support act six?

Act seven – Do a kind act....
for yourself

This act encourages you to take time out and do something that replenishes your soul. You might enjoy taking a relaxing warm bath or a power nap in the afternoon. Just make it happen.

For those that are time poor, can you delegate some of your load to free up some *me* time?

If you are not overly committed, can you step up and help some-one else who is?

Be kind to yourself, but also be kind to each other. What will you do this week to support act seven?

Thursday

This week I have taken
the time to do things
that make me feel
uplifted.
I really enjoyed my
walk along the beach.

Note to self ...
Do more things
that make me feel

relaxed and happy.

* Walk more

* Stay off social
media

* Read more books

Journaling is a perfect self-love activity.
Spend time reflecting on the seven daily acts of self-love.
Be open and honest with your journal entry and write from
the heart.

What did you learn about yourself this week?

What did you learn about each other this week?

What is your favourite act?

What will you do next week to support your self-care?

What are you grateful for this week?

"

The best way to
love and honor your family is...
love and honor yourself fully.

Week 5
Nourish
Your Mind

Your goal this week-
To fill your mind with positive seeds

Over the next seven days, everyone participating in
Project Shine must complete the following –

Create ten personal I AM affirmations.
(follow the I AM worksheet for guidance)

Create the affirmations to support your individual
personality and requirements.

Schedule at least one family dinner to discuss why you chose
your particular affirmations.

Say your individual affirmations with conviction
ten times every morning upon rising and ten times each night
before you fall asleep for the next seven days or forever if
you want.

Please note-
No phones or electronic devices allowed during any of these
activities. During your family catch-ups, be fully present and
engaged.

Your mind is like a garden bed. If you plant positive seeds in it, your whole being will flourish. If you are continuously planting negative seeds it is obvious what will happen.

Take a moment to ask yourself the following question. What are you planting in your mind? Flowers or weeds.

This week's task focusses on planting positive seeds into your mind every day. A simple and effective way to plant these seeds, is through reciting affirmations.

Affirmations are positive, specific statements that help you disrupt negative thought patterns.

Have you ever thought about the power of the words I AM?

Even deeper, have you ever stopped to acknowledge the I AM statements you are perhaps thinking and verbalizing about yourself?

Think about that for a moment and, hey, be honest......
What I AM statements are YOU running through your mind right now?

"The words I AM have the power to make our dreams come true." - Dr Wayne Dyer.

I AM is the single most powerful statement in the English Language. What you put after these two words creates your world, reality, and your future. If you want your whole life to improve, it is important to pay attention to your thoughts and your language.

Why is it helpful to recite affirmations?

Well, they motivate us. They influence the subconscious mind and they have the power to change the way you think and behave. Positive statements make you feel more optimistic and can put you in a better place to transform your inner and external worlds.

It is important to create affirmations that resonate with you. When you create your ten daily affirmations, make sure they feel authentic and achievable. You can use the following examples on the next page as a guideline.

I AM healthy, I AM positive, I AM inspiring,
I AM happy, I AM creative,
I AM resourceful, I AM persistent,
I AM resilient, I AM love, I AM loved,
I AM grateful, I AM blessed , I AM committed to my goals,
I AM responsible for my life.

I AM a terrific mother, I AM a terrific father,
I AM a supportive sister, I AM a caring brother,
I AM able to help others, I AM determined to succeed,
I AM worthy of the best in life, I AM learning from my
mistakes, I AM getting stronger every day.

Now it's your turn

Creating I AM statements is a powerful exercise. By attempting to fill your mind with all that is right with you and your world, you can quite literally change your life.

The task at hand is to create *your* own ten affirmations. Repeat your personal affirmations at night before you fall asleep and as soon as you wake up.

Remember to create affirmations that feel relatable to you. This is important. You must feel confident and comfortable reciting them.

Write them in your journal or even better place them on a sheet of paper and display them somewhere prominent so you see and say them often.

Your mission with this task is…..

to plant hundreds of positive seeds in your mind and grow hundreds of beautiful thought flowers.

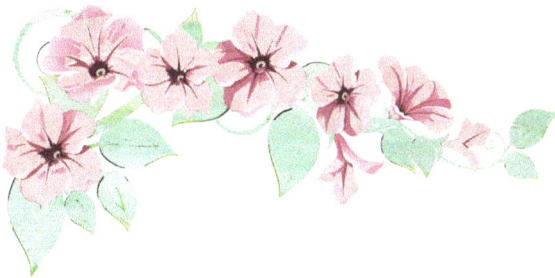

Write your ten affirmations in your journal. Get to it!

Repetition is the key to making affirmations effective.

Your subconscious mind is most receptive to your thoughts, words, and messages in the final minutes before you fall asleep and again during the first hour of the morning, so commit to reciting your affirmations morning and night.

State them as though you are already in possession of the outcome. If you feel comfortable, share your affirmations with one another. You never know, one of your affirmations may inspire one of your loved ones to plant that same beautiful seed.

Affirmation Tips

Make sure your affirmations are believable to you.
For example, you might feel comfortable saying,
"I AM confident."

Perhaps the following is more relatable to you.
" I AM struggling with my self-confidence, but I am
working on improving this every single day."

Combine your daily affirmations with action.
Make sure you are taking the necessary steps
daily to empower yourself.

Change your affirmations regularly and modify
them as you grow.

Display your positive statements everywhere.
Bathroom mirrors are perfect for displaying
positive affirmation post-it notes!

Reflection and journaling - Week 5

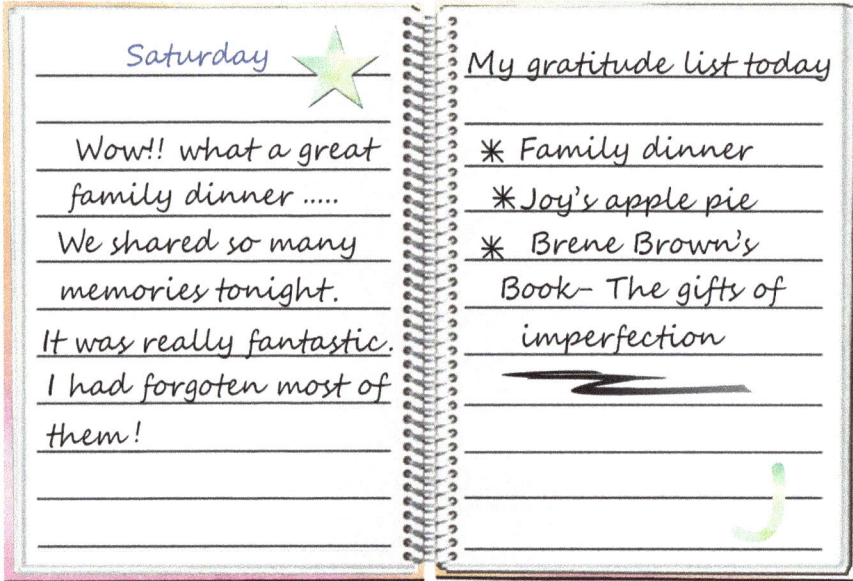

Saturday ⭐

Wow!! what a great
family dinner .....
We shared so many
memories tonight.
It was really fantastic.
I had forgoten most of
them!

My gratitude list today

* Family dinner
* Joy's apple pie
* Brene Brown's
  Book- The gifts of
  imperfection

By now, you should be an expert at journaling.
I don't even need to remind you how to make an entry.
GO FOR IT!

What did you learn about yourself this week?

What did you learn about each other this week?

What is your favourite I AM statement and why?

What are you grateful for this week?

66

Who am I?

I am me and I am perfectly fine with
that!

Week 6
Soul Food

Your goal this week -
Cook with love and good energy

Over the next seven days, everyone participating in
Project Shine must complete the following -

Plan and prepare a beautiful meal to share together.

Everyone is to participate in the creation of
The Menu | The Meal | The Dinner Table
The Conversation.

The task leader should allocate jobs to ensure that
everyone takes part in bringing this meal to fruition. Make
sure you reserve a large chunk of time for this special
activity.

It can be breakfast, brunch, lunch, dinner or supper.
It is your choice.

It doesn't need to be complicated,
just healthy and made with love.

Please note-
No phones or electronic devices allowed during any of these
activities. During your family catch-ups, be fully present
and engaged.

The secret ingredient is always love...

I can give you a million reasons why I like to cook a meal for my family by myself. It is quicker, simpler and definitely less messy. However, the benefits of planning and cooking a beautiful meal together and sharing it as a family far outweighs all of those millions of reasons.

When we prepare a beautiful meal together, it allows us to reconnect, converse, bond, and support one another. It also allows us to create beautiful memories we can all share for a lifetime.

Cooking and preparing a meal together also makes us more mindful of the nutritional value of food. It teaches us valuable cooking skills. It allows us to disconnect from technology and engage with one another. It reminds us to be grateful.

Sadly, many families in the world go hungry on a daily basis. Sharing a meal together allows us the opportunity to practice gratitude and acknowledge how blessed we are.

It seems that we are in danger of losing this priceless and precious tradition of eating together. More and more families eat on the run or on the couch and even in the car.

Project Shine is about connection and I urge you to enjoy a family dinner at least once a week or as often as you can.

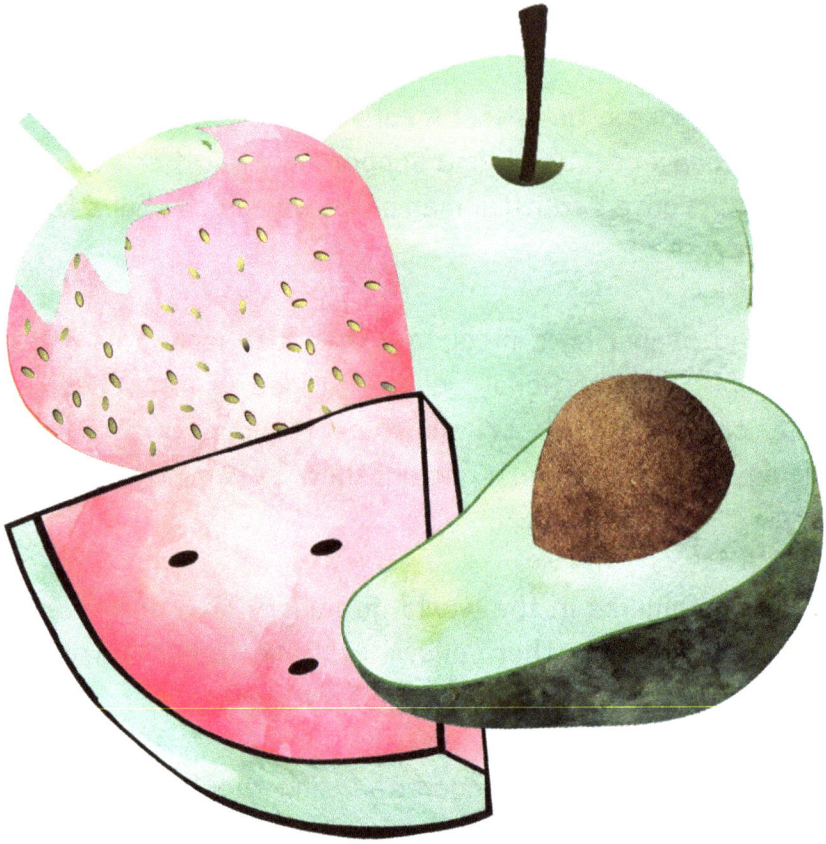

The Soul Food Experience
Your task this week is to plan and prepare a meal together

Allocate a few hours where everyone can
come together to take part in this task..

Your mission with this task....

To create, prepare and share a delicious meal.
It can be brunch, lunch, dinner or supper.
There are no rules.

Decide on a beautiful, healthy meal option. It doesn't have to
be complicated. For example, making pizzas from scratch and
creating interesting toppings can be simple, healthy and fun.

Follow my recipe…..

Create food that is good for the soul
Food should be colorful, healthy and delicious.
It should taste good, look good and be good for you.
Always choose to nourish yourself with foods that will make
you shine.

Prepare your meal with love
Whatever your role in preparing the family meal –
chop, cut, shred and prepare lovingly.
Put your heart and soul into it and do your part with gusto
and flair. Everyone should get involved and put their best
energy into the mixture.

Set a table fit for royalty
Create a beautiful table setting. Use your best china.
Don't wait for a special occasion. Every day is special.
Place flowers or candles on the table.
Set the mood – one of calm, peace, love and appreciation for
the opportunity to engage together over a beautiful meal.

Enjoy
Make sure that there are no phones or computers on or at
the table. This is a time to savor the food,
the conversation and one another.

Gratitude
Give thanks. You have enjoyed a beautiful meal. You are
surrounded by loved ones. The most cherished memories are
made around a gathered table.

Healthy Tips

Commit to only shopping the perimeter of your supermarket for your groceries. This is where you will find all the fresh produce.
The pre-packaged and processed foods are in the central aisles.

Eat a rainbow every day.

Fresh herbs and spices have healing properties. Use them abundantly.

Learn to be mindful when eating.

Allow your stomach and brain receptors the privilege of catching up with each other before you decide that you need more food.
Chances are you are already full.

Reflection and journaling – week six

Monday

This week I have struggled a little bit with everything !! I've been really tired. I plan to go to bed earlier every night from now on.

* Get up earlier
* Go for an early morning run
* Have a healthy breakfast
* Drink more water

I hope you have enjoyed this week's soul food experience. It is now time to write how you are feeling in your journal.

What did you learn about yourself this week?

What did you learn about each other this week?

How did you feel about your contribution to the Soul Food Experience?

Did you enjoy the meal?

What are you grateful for this week?

66

Together.....
we make a family

Week 7
Inhale...Exhale

Your goal this week-
Pay attention to your breathing

Over the next seven days, everyone participating in
Project Shine must complete the following -

Schedule a family dinner to discuss ways you can
incorporate some of your favourite activities from
Project Shine into the upcoming week.

For example, you might create new affirmations or
schedule more daily acts of self-love.
Perhaps you will share another soul food experience.
Together, create a week filled with positive activities.

Commit to practicing three cycles of deep breathing first
thing in the morning, at least once during the afternoon and
then again in the evening.

If the opportunity arises, practice your breathing
cycles together.

No phones or electronic devices allowed during any of these
activities. During your family catch-ups, be fully present
and engaged.

Breathing is something we all do and yet it is something we rarely pay much attention to. We take almost fifteen thousand breaths a day without even thinking about them.

Focussing on your breathing is one of the most powerful ways to calm your mind, body, and spirit. It is an essential tool for supporting wellness. Deep breathing counters the effects of stress by slowing the heart rate and lowering blood pressure.

Often just getting back to the basics and taking a holistic, simple approach to life can bring about huge benefits.

Throughout the course of the day when you feel
stressed or overwhelmed, remember to
take three deep breaths and
breathe away all of your tension.

Practice the following breathing exercise
three times a day, every day for the next seven days.

Get into the habit of deep breathing whenever
you are feeling overwhelmed.

Sit up straight and close your eyes.

Place your hands on your belly.

Slowly inhale through your nose and pay attention to
the feeling as the breath starts to fill up your
abdomen and spread to the top of your head.
Inhale to the count of three while you are
doing this.

Once you feel that your abdomen is fully expanded,
hold the breath for three more counts.

Finally, reverse the process as you exhale through your
mouth for a further count of three.

Do this simple exercise for three cycles.

Reflection and journaling-week seven

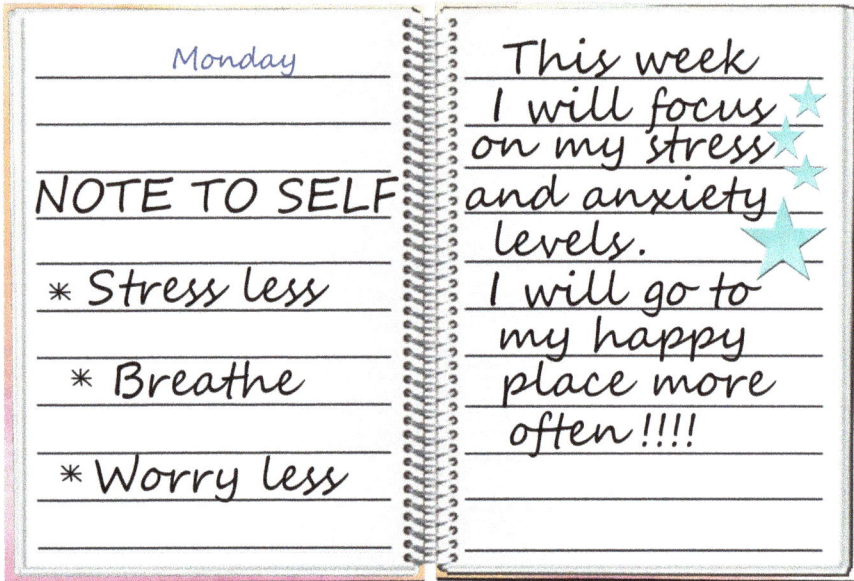

Monday

NOTE TO SELF

* Stress less

* Breathe

* Worry less

This week
I will focus
on my stress
and anxiety
levels.
I will go to
my happy
place more
often !!!!

Journaling should be an enjoyable experience for you now.
You have been expressing your thoughts and words into
your journal for seven weeks. Read through all of your
entries and acknowledge how far you have come.

What did you learn about yourself this week?

What did you learn about each other this week?

What other activities make you feel relaxed?

What are you grateful for this week?

66

Every breath you take is a gift

Week 8
Quiet The
Mind

Your goal this week –
Quiet and calm your mind

Over the next seven days, everyone participating in
Project Shine must complete the following –

Schedule a family dinner and select some of your favourite
activities from past chapters and repeat them. Use your
imagination to modify the activities and change them up.
Create a positively inspiring week.

Practice some form of meditation together three times this
week for at least five minutes per session.
If you can invest more time into this activity, go for it.

No phones or electronic devices allowed during any of these
activities. During your family catch-ups be fully present and
engaged.

The goal of meditation is to evoke a feeling of peace and calm in your mind, body, and spirit. The more you practice meditation, the easier it is to maintain a beautiful feeling of inner peace. The calmness and clarity that results from daily meditation will eventually become your new state of being. What's not to LOVE about that?

Tip one- Create a zen space

Create an area in your home where you can sit and be still with each other for at least five minutes each day. Place a mat and some cushions on the floor. This little spot should evoke peace and stimulate the senses so go wild and burn scented candles and oils in this space. You can even play some relaxing, instrumental, calming music.

Make sure everyone closes their eyes and focusses on their breathing and if you can, sit cross-legged on the floor in your zen space. To begin with, allocate just five minutes daily to this practice. You can always increase it over time. Before you know it, you will be meditating for twenty minutes every day.

Tip two-Visualize

If you still read with your children, perhaps a bedtime story could be replaced with a beautiful guided visualization. You can take your child on a magical, peaceful journey together. Get your child to close their eyes and then gently guide them to visualize in their mind's eye your special adventure.

Maybe you can go on a magical walk through an enchanted, peaceful forest. Whatever you choose, guided imagery is a perfect way to find peace after a hectic day.

If you are taking part in Project Shine and have outgrown storytelling and reading together, get creative and take it in turns to create a guided imagery session that you can share with one another. Go wild with your visualization.

Tip three- Guided visual meditations

There are hundreds of meditations available for free online. You can even find them on YouTube. There are specially created guided meditations that offer all sorts of experiences, so open your mind and your heart and explore the many options available to us all.

Meditation Tips

Breathe naturally when meditating.

Don't get caught up in the HOW TO
part of meditating. Just relax into it.

Let thoughts come in and let them flow out.
Start with five minutes a day and increase
it over time.

Meditation is a beautiful way to still the
mind and settle that annoying constant
mind chatter. When you stop this
internal dialogue, the mind can settle.

Quite simply: meditation gives you
peace of mind.

Find time to meditate every day.

There is an old zen saying –
" You should sit in meditation for twenty minutes
a day unless you are too busy and then you
should sit for an hour."

Reflection and journaling-week eight

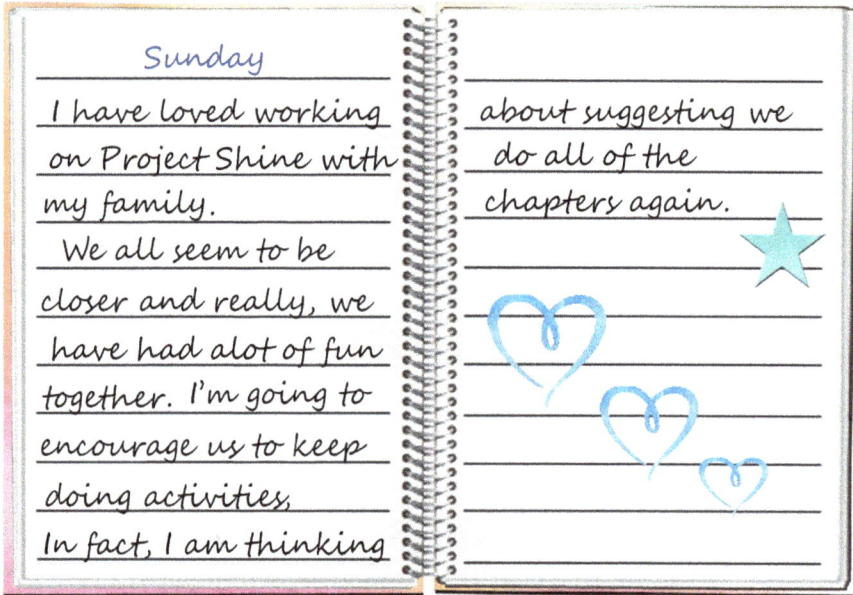

Sunday

I have loved working
on Project Shine with
my family.
We all seem to be
closer and really, we
have had alot of fun
together. I'm going to
encourage us to keep
doing activities,
In fact, I am thinking

about suggesting we
do all of the
chapters again.

I hope you continue to journal long after
you have finished Project Shine.
You should be so proud of all you have achieved during your
Project Shine journey.

What did you learn about yourself during the last eight
weeks of working on Project Shine?

What did you learn about each other?

How have YOU changed because of Project Shine?

The Project Shine Manifesto

I promise to be kind to myself every day.
I am committed to prioritizing my self-care.
I am responsible for nourishing myself in mind,
body, and spirit. I will devote the time and energy
daily into managing my wellness because...
I AM WORTH IT.
I am strong enough and smart enough to achieve
my dreams. I am the STAR of my life and I
will shine my light and encourage others to
do the same.
I HONOR myself and I HONOR my family.
I have the power to change my thoughts and actions
minute by minute. I am committed to sharing good
energy with my loved ones and with the world.

Today and every day, I choose to live in the spirit of
gratitude. The love in my heart and the power in my
soul fuels my belief that.....anything is possible.
From this day forth, I will always SHINE.

Love Notes

Little gifts of inspiration and motivation

Receive your daily love note by randomly selecting a page from my love notes section each morning.

Your face tells your life story. Your scars reflect your battles and triumphs. For many, these scars symbolize survival. Your lines and wrinkles are imprints of a life well lived. They represent laughter, experience, and wisdom.

Why are we so intent on removing them?

You are BEAUTIFUL...OWN IT.

It doesn't matter what age you are, remember...

I am not beautiful like you; I am beautiful like me.

Your love note today is - You have the power

You have the power to set your mood for the day as soon as you open your eyes. When you wake, your brain is coming out of a slower brainwave state.

What does that mean?

It means that your mind is receptive to your ideas and thoughts. Before you get out of bed, decide what sort of day you will have.

Are you going to have a good day or a great day?

You create your mindset for the whole day while you are still in this slower brain state by making a conscious choice.

Always remember…

YOU hold the power to create an extraordinary life.

Your love note today is -
You are your own source of happiness

Think about what would make you happy today.
In order to experience more positive emotions, we need to do
more positive things. Whether those positive things are
activities from Project Shine or your own ideas...
for example - making time to have a catch-up with friends,
a run along the beach or any activity that allows you to
experience happiness, remember, happiness comes from your
own actions.
Come on....get happy.

Your love note today is -
Just breathe

When you breathe in today,
fill yourself with gratitude – gratitude for your life.
When you breathe out today - let go of all the unnecessary
demands that you place on yourself.
Remember….just breathe.

Your love note today is -
True authenticity is golden

NO-ONE can truly capture the true genius of what YOU do and what YOU stand for. When you are not being true to yourself, you are not following your life's purpose, so don't try to copy anyone else.
Be fearless in sharing your true authenticity with the world. You were born to be real.
Believe in yourself and always remember...
No-one does YOU better than YOU.
The world is in desperate need of your uniqueness.

Your love note today is - Forgive

It can seem almost impossible to forgive someone when you are hurting. Forgiving someone does not mean forgetting a wrongful action or excusing how hurtful it perhaps was. Forgiveness is a choice and a gift you give to yourself. We forgive because it has an enormous impact on the state of our mind, body, and spirit. Don't underestimate the power of forgiveness and the enormous release you will feel when you practice this ultimate act of self-love.

PS.

While you are at it...

forgive yourself if you need to.

Your love note today - Seize the day

Embrace this brand new day and every day with purpose. Just as the world continues to turn, a new day brings endless opportunities. A new day generates renewed energy and hope so choose how you will respond to the day's events by welcoming each new day with optimism. Make this day amazing.

Your love note today is -
Let go

Punishing yourself for anything in your past just keeps you
connected to the problem. Give yourself permission today
to release anything that does not support you in a loving way.
Letting go does not mean you are giving up.
Letting go allows you to feel peace.

Your love note today is -
You are supported

Always remember -
If you get lost, the people who love you
will come and find you.......
You can be certain of that.

Your love note today is –
There is no such thing as failure

Challenges, hurdles, and struggles are a part of life.
They teach us valuable lessons and realistically; they are
just detour signs along life's road encouraging each one of
us to find another way to succeed.

Your love note today is -
Honor yourself

You are sacred and divine.
Never forget how miraculous you are.
In this moment, as you read this love note,
commit to honoring yourself.
Positive and loving thoughts, healthy choices every day,
dancing in the moonlight, saluting the sun,
engaging with people who respect you.
Always follow your heart.
You are a divine human being.

Your love note today is - Dream big

Einstein, Dr. Martin Luther King, Oprah Winfrey,
Plato, Marie Curie, Walt Disney, Waldo Emerson,
Steve Jobs, The Wright Brothers, Amelia Earhart,

Insert your name here_____

The process of dreaming and creating is awe-inspiring.
Taking something like a thought or a dream and
manifesting it into the physical world is
a pretty incredible thing.
Some of the world's most inspiring ideas were sparked by
a thought or a dream.
If you can imagine it, you can create it.

Your love note today is - Believe in yourself

You can achieve anything, absolutely anything.
There are no limits on what you can achieve.
The only limits are the ones you impose upon yourself.
Dream, believe and take action every day.
Back yourself.

Your love note today is -
Make changes, not excuses

Be thankful that you can change your life's course in a
heartbeat, because if you think about it……
YOU CAN.

Your love note today is -
You are ENOUGH

Today's love note is a reminder that......
YOU ARE ENOUGH.
This love note invites you to stop and acknowledge all of
your achievements to date and accept that you alone are
enough. You have nothing to prove to anybody so with
that thought in mind, remember, you are *more* than enough.

Your love note today is -
Give yourself permission to rest

By giving yourself permission to STOP, and by accepting that rest is a highly productive activity, you can come back to your tasks, goals, dreams and plans with renewed energy and insight. Take time out today to rest and relax.

Your love note today is -
Shower the people you love with love and more love

Never waste an opportunity to tell someone you love them or appreciate them. In the blink of an eye, life can change so forgive often and love with all of your heart.

Your love note today is –
Give thanks

Gratitude will make you abundant.
When we acknowledge our blessings,
we experience a profound shift in all areas of life.
Gratitude requires no money and very little effort.
When you give thanks and practice gratitude, you will be
blessed with true wealth but in a much deeper sense.
What are you grateful for right now?

Your love note today is -
Soften your focus

If you soften your focus, you will find life's journey will be much gentler. Focussing softly and taking a calm, gentle approach towards every situation before reacting allows you time to evaluate the event. Shifting your vision to be more emotionally intelligent, empathetic and caring will open up a whole new level of mindfulness.

Softly, softly.

Your love note today is -
Paint a beautiful picture

When you paint a picture of what you want your life to look like, and when you can see that picture in your mind's eye, you can bring this vision to life. Wellness, fitness, peace, more energy, nothing is off limits when it comes to coloring your world and creating your work of art.
Once you have painted your masterpiece onto the canvas of your mind, be sure to take time to focus on it every day.
Embrace the colors, the richness and feel the joy that this painting brings. Take the steps to make that painting and all of its colors spill over into your physical world.
Your future is a blank canvas and you can create any picture you want. Make it beautiful.

I hope you always SHINE
Jo Ettles

www.ingramcontent.com/pod-product-compliance
Lightning Source LLC
Chambersburg PA
CBHW061956090426
42811CB00006B/960